YANKEE STADIUM IN YOUR POCKET

The Yankee Fan's Guide to Yankee Stadium

Kevin T. Dame

Published by Baseball Direct
Central Falls, RI

Design by Christine Dame Yoshida
Layout by Janice Garsh and Chrystal Baudot
Illustrations by Ryoji Yoshida, Kevin Dame, and
Christine Dame Yoshida.

First Printing
Printed in the United States of America

This book may be ordered directly from the publisher by
sending a check or money order for $6.95 per book plus
$2.00 shipping and handling to:
Baseball Direct, P.O. Box 6463, Central Falls, RI 02863.

Contents

Chapter Three: Play Ball!

Chapter Four: Post-Game Tips

Chapter Five: Life Beyond Yankee Stadium

Chapter Six: Fanhood Challenge

Preface

Any sports fan worth his salt is familiar with the expression "the house that Ruth built." It refers to Yankee Stadium, once upon a time the world's most spectacular sports complex. It now serves as a veritable baseball shrine, as decades of baseball history have unfolded within its walls.

This book is about Yankee Stadium, one of the remaining ball parks from baseball's early years. In an era of fabricated nostalgia, Yankee Stadium serves as a reminiscent reminder of the way baseball used to be. A night at Yankee Stadium is probably little different than one fifty years ago when Joe DiMaggio was terrorizing opposing American League pitchers.

This book is not about boring history or "who cares" trivia. It is a user's guide to Yankee Stadium, written for you the Yankee Stadium parishioner, to help you get the most out of your experience at the game. Whether it's a helpful tip on where to park your car, or a review of the "Yankee Stadium Beer Rules," you'll be coached step by step through the entire experience.

I hope that you take this guide with you whenever you venture off to the Stadium. I also urge you to fill out the survey in the back of this book with your own ideas and tips on how to enjoy the Yankee Stadium experience, and send it to our PO Box address. Your unique perspective will help us to continually improve this guide and help fans enjoy their experience all the more.

As you join the millions of fans who enter Yankee Stadium this summer, use this guide to its fullest and you'll be guaranteed a great time.

CHAPTER ONE

YANKEE STADIUM BASICS

Yankee Stadium Oath

Before we begin, every Yankee Stadium visitor must learn the basic rule of fanhood – the Yankee Stadium oath:

> On my honor, I promise to cheer on my Yankees, to devour hot dogs and peanuts, to properly execute the wave, and to soak in the fresh air, smells, sights, and sounds of Yankee Stadium, until I am truly at peace.

Baseball psychics have determined that the ghosts of Ruth, Gehrig, and other Yankee greats are pleased when an entire stadium of Yankee fans recite this oath before games. Please recite the oath before the game (under your breath if you must) for the sake of good cosmic karma. Do it for the Babe!

Yankee Stadium: History 101

During the summer of 1920, New York Giants manager John McGraw watched in anger as their cross-town rival, the New York Yankees (who played their home games at the Giants' Polo grounds), began to outdraw the Giants. Led by Babe Ruth's .376 average and unheard of 54 home runs, the Yankees drew 1.3 million fans at the Polo Grounds as fans clamored to see the Yankees' new star. As a result, the Giants demanded that the Yankees hit the road and build their own stadium, and Yankees owner Jacob Ruppert jumped at the opportunity to build what would become baseball's most famous stadium. The team began the process of searching for a construction site for a new stadium, and ultimately settled on a spot in the western section of the Bronx. In less than a year, Yankee Stadium was built: a magnificent, triple-decked structure designed to showcase Ruth and other star players pillaged from the rival Boston Red Sox. Opening day occurred on April 18, 1923, and the Yankees defeated the Red Sox 4-1 behind (you guessed it) Babe Ruth's first home run of the season. Yankee Stadium soon became known as "The House That Ruth Built."

The original design consisted of three concrete decks extending from home plate out to the left and right-field corners, a single deck in left field, and wooden bleachers in center and right fields. In 1928, second and third decks were added to left field. Further upgrades occurred, as the wooden bleachers were replaced with concrete in 1937, and auxiliary scoreboards were added in the late 1940's.

In its early years, Yankee stadium was a quirky place. The team erected a green screen in centerfield, which provided Yankee hitters with a better hitting background. Of course, when the opposing hitters  stepped to the plate the Yankees would often remove the screen, leaving the visiting slugger with a hitting background of white-shirted bleacher fans. Years later, deep left center field would feature three, in-play stone monuments which honored Yankee great's Gehrig, Huggins, and Ruth. During one game, manager Casey Stengel watched as a well hit ball sailed past the Yankee centerfielder and rattled around among the monuments. As the beleaguered fielder struggled to corral the elusive ball, legend has it that Stengel yelled, "Ruth, Gehrig, Huggins, someone throw that darned ball in here, now!"

Yankee Stadium's most dramatic renovation occurred during a two year period from 1974-1975, during which the Yankees played their home games at nearby Shea Stadium. During this major undertaking the field dimensions were altered, the famous monuments were relocated to Monument Park behind the left field fence, and most of the stadium's beautiful copper, art deco frieze was removed from the roof facade. (Some of this frieze was preserved and today hangs above the bleachers in centerfield).

Yankee Stadium's largest crowd occurred in 1928, as 85,265 fans packed the place to watch the Yankees face the powerful Philadelphia Athletics. The smallest crowd ever to take in a game in the Bronx occurred in 1966, as 413 fans willed themselves to endure a game against the Chicago White Sox. Yankee Stadium's current capacity stands at 57,545.

Season Time-Line

The true baseball fan realizes that even though the season officially ends in October, in reality it continues on throughout the winter and spring. Your time away from Yankee Stadium during the "off-season" is a time to reflect on the previous season, speculate on possible trades and free-agent acquisitions, and to mentally psyche yourself up for the next season. By March, you should be experiencing serious withdrawal pains and eagerly anticipating opening day at Yankee Stadium!

Yankee Fan's
Twelve-Month Planner

January
Winter Ball in
S. America

February
Players prep
for spring
training

March
Spring Training
Games!

April
Opening
Day!

May
Yankees pull
out in front!

June
College
Baseball
draft

July
All-Star
Game!

August
Listen to
Yankees games
on beach

September
Pennant
Fever!

October
Playoffs and
World Series

November
Debate trades
with friends

December
Winter
Meetings:
New Players!

Yankee Stadium Fast-Facts

For those of you who are trapped in the fast-paced lifestyle of the 90's, you need the most important information boiled down to a simple, easy to read format that even a chimpanzee could understand. (For the people who typically read USA Today and only read the blurbs on the bottom left of the front page, these FAST-FACTS are for you!)

Yankee Stadium
161st St. and River Avenue
Bronx, NY. 10451
Ticket Information: (718)293-6000
www.yankeees.com

Home games: 81 games (April to October)
Game times: 1:05 pm (day), 7:05 pm (night)
TV coverage: WNYW channel 5 for 50 games
(the rest on Fox and MSG network)
Radio Coverage: WABC 770 AM

CHAPTER TWO

PRE-GAME PREP

Selecting a Game

The art of selecting the perfect game is based upon five important factors. Whether it be for your family, the date you're trying to impress, or a business client, considering these five factors will help make your time at Yankee Stadium all the more enjoyable:

1. Weather and time of day
2. Time of season
3. The opponent
4. Pitching match-ups
5. Yankee promotions.

Weather

It's most important to be comfortable! The prospects of shivering in the face of cold, gusting winds, squinting through your rain-soaked glasses, or passing out due to 90-degree temperatures can all be eliminat- ed if you dress properly for the weather and time of day. In April, and again in September, you may need a winter jacket, a sweater, and possibly a hat, gloves, and even thermal underwear. Remember, you'll be sitting outside in one place for three hours. For those of you who think that drinking alcohol will keep you warm (college students, pay attention) — you're wrong! The alcohol slows down your metabolism and opens up the pores in your skin. You could actually get hypothermia!

In the middle of the season, during New York's warmest weather, shorts and T-shirts suffice during the day, while a wind-breaker is usually a good idea to have with you during night games. Certain areas of the stadium (especially the bleachers) are exposed to strong sunshine, so during the summer make sure to bring a supply of sunscreen. Loge and main reserved seats are mostly shielded from the rain, and during a rain delay you will be protected. However, if you are in an unprotected zone (bleachers), make sure you bring a small umbrella just in case of rain. (See "Picking the Best Place to Sit" on page 24 for more information.) Even when rain is forecasted — a common occurrence in New York summers — grab a wind breaker and umbrella and head to the stadium. It's still worth going because many games are still played after a short delay. You can get a better idea of the likelihood of a game being cancelled by calling the Yankees at (718) 293–6000, or by listening to WABC 770 AM on the radio for the latest weather information.

Time of Season

The time of season strongly influences ticket availability, the size of crowds, and the general atmosphere inside the stadium. The first month of the season is an exciting time for fans (especially opening day), but seats are a bit easier to get due to the colder weather. During the dog days of summer (late July through August), games are often sold out, yet many fans lose a little interest and turn their attention to barbecues, trips to the beach, and members of the opposite sex. In September, Yankee Stadium can be slower if the team is out of contention, but is buzzing with excitement and filled to the brim with rabid fans if the Yankees are battling for the divisional crown. Because of Yankee Stadium's allure and charm, its slowest moments are still characterized by healthy attendance.

Opponent

"Who are the Yankees playing tonight?"— a common question asked by fans considering a game. Games against arch-rivals (Red Sox, Orioles) are more exciting and sought after than games against other teams (Tigers, Twins). In fact, attending a Red Sox - Yankees game at Yankee Stadium is one of the most intense experiences in sports.

Pitching Match-Ups

Predicting a game's starting pitcher can be done a few days before the game. This can be accomplished if you know the team pitching rotation. For example, if the Yankees' starting rotation is (1) Clemens, (2) Cone, (3) Hernandez, (4) Petitte, and (5) Irabu, and Clemens pitched on Monday night, then you can predict with reasonable certainty that Hernandez will pitch on Wednesday night, two games after Clemens. Star pitchers are always worth going out of your way to see if you appreciate good pitching. If you want to see lots of hits and runs, your best bet is to pick games with the worst pitchers. While the pitching match-ups add to the flavor of the game, most fans generally select a game without concern for the pitchers.

You can also read the Pitching Match-Ups in the Newspaper: In the newspaper sports page, look for a section entitled "Today's Probable Pitchers/Latest Line" (usually found below the standings). Quite a bit of information can be found in this section, including the game times. Most games begin at 7:05 p.m. on weeknights, and 1:05 p.m. during the day.

Beginning with the left column, you can identify the teams playing one another (the first is the home team). Next to each team is the name of the pitcher starting the game. In parentheses next to each

TODAY'S PROBABLE PITCHERS

AMERICAN LEAGUE

	Time	Line	1998 W-L	1998 ERA	Team Rec.	1998 vs. opp. W-L	IP	ERA	Last 3 starts W-L	IP	ERA	AHWG
BOS Martinez (R)	1:35	-220	8-2	3.31	10-5	0-0	0.0	0.00	2-1	17.2	6.62	14.8
At TB Johnson (R)			2-3	5.67	6-4	0-0	0.0	0.00	0-1	11.1	8.74	15.1
KC Pichardo (R)	1:05	-115	2-6	5.96	4-3	0-0	0.0	0.00	2-1	16.0	3.94	13.5
At DET Harriger (R)			0-1	6.75	0-1	0-0	0.0	0.00	0-1	5.1	6.75	15.2
TOR Hentgen (R)	1:35	-115	7-4	4.35	8-7	0-0	0.0	0.00	0-0	20.1	3.54	13.7
At BAL Ponson (R)			1-4	5.28	1-3	0-0	0.0	0.00	1-2	18.1	2.95	11.3
MIN Morgan (R)	2:05	-115	3-2	3.95	6-8	0-0	0.0	0.00	1-1	16.0	3.38	12.4
At CHI Bere (R)			3-6	5.94	5-9	0-0	0.0	0.00	1-2	14.2	7.36	17.2
OAK Oquist (R)	4:35	-145	4-3	5.13	6-8	1-0	7.2	2.35	2-0	19.0	5.68	11.8
At SEA Swift (R)			6-4	4.54	6-7	0-0	0.0	0.00	2-1	15.1	1.17	11.2
NY Irabu (R)	8:05	-120	6-2	1.68	7-4	0-0	0.0	0.00	2-1	20.1	2.21	11.1
At CLE Colon (R)			6-4	2.73	7-7	0-0	0.0	0.00	1-2	25.2	1.40	7.0
TEX Perisho (L)	8:05	-140	0-1	23.14	0-1	0-0	0.0	0.00	0-1	2.1	23.14	30.9
At ANA Dickson (R)			7-4	5.43	5-4	0-0	0.0	0.00	3-0	21.0	3.00	10.3

NATIONAL LEAGUE

	Time	Line	1998 W-L	1998 ERA	Team Rec.	1998 vs. opp. W-L	IP	ERA	Last 3 starts W-L	IP	ERA	AHWG
ATL Neagle (L)	1:35	-170	8-4	3.18	10-5	1-0	7.0	1.29	1-2	24.0	3.75	9.0
At MON Hermanson (R)			4-6	3.20	4-7	0-0	0.0	0.00	1-2	17.0	1.59	10.6
FLA Fontenot (R)	1:40	-350	0-4	8.14	0-5	0-0	0.0	0.00	0-2	17.0	6.35	15.9
At NY Leiter (L)			8-3	1.53	8-5	0-0	0.0	0.00	3-0	21.0	0.86	9.0
PIT Loaiza (R)	2:05	-150	4-3	4.73	4-6	0-0	0.0	0.00	1-2	17.0	4.24	14.3
At MIL			6-5	4.06	7-8	1-0	13.0	0.69	1-1	19.0	4.26	11.8
ARI Daal (L)	2:10	-150	3-4	2.82	5-3	0-0	0.0	0.00	2-1	23.0	2.74	10.6
At St.L Acevedo (R)			2-1	4.68	2-2	0-0	2.0	9.00	1-0	13.0	4.85	11.8
PHI Green (R)	2:20	-165	4-4	5.21	6-8	0-0	0.0	0.00	1-0	18.2	6.27	14.0
At CHI Trachsel (R)			6-3	4.04	9-5	0-0	0.0	0.00	0-2	19.2	6.41	13.7
CIN Harnisch (R)	2:35	-130	6-2	2.78	7-8	0-0	0.0	0.00	2-1	21.0	1.71	9.4
At HOU Schourek (L)			3-5	4.70	3-5	0-0	0.0	0.00	1-2	17.0	4.24	11.6
LA Park (R)	3:05	-110	5-4	4.63	8-7	0-0	0.0	0.00	1-1	21.0	3.43	10.7
At COL Jones (L)			1-2	5.55	3-2	0-0	0.0	0.00	0-2	17.0	7.41	16.9
SD Brown (R)	4:05	-120	7-3	2.84	10-6	1-0	9.0	0.00	2-0	20.0	4.50	14.0
At SF Hershiser (R)			6-4	3.27	10-5	0-0	0.0	0.00	1-1	16.1	4.96	17.6

KEY: TEAM REC - Team's record in games started by today's pitcher. AHWG - Average hits and walks allowed per game in last 3 starts.

pitcher is R or L, indicating right or left-hander. The time of the game is shown next, along with the odds for those confident enough to bet on a base-ball game. The next two columns show the pitchers' performance up to that point in the season. W-L indicates the pitchers' record (wins and losses), and ERA indicates their earned run averages (ERA is basically the number of runs the pitcher is yielding on average in a 9-inning game). The rest of the columns provide information about each team's record when the pitcher starts the game, the pitcher's success (or failure) against the opponent this year, the pitcher's performance in his last three starts, and (for the number-crunching rotisserie baseball fans) the average number of hits and walks the pitcher has yielded per 9 innings in his last three starts. The acronym for this statistic – AHWG – is surprisingly similar to the sound a pitcher makes after giving up a home run.

Yankee Stadium Promotions

The Yankees also offer special promotions through-out the year, mostly targeted at younger fans (This means complimentary souvenirs!). Popular promotions include Beanie Babies Day, Cap Day, Batting Helmet Bank Day, and Tote Bag Day. Call the Yankees Ticket Office for more information (see Ordering Tickets section).

Ordering Tickets

Yankees Clubhouse Stores

You can buy your Yankees tickets from any of four Yankees Clubhouse Stores: In Manhattan, 110 E. 59th Street, between Lexington and Park, (212) 758-7844; also in Manhattan, 393 Fifth Ave, between 36th and 37th Streets, (212) 685-4693; also in Manhattan, 8 Fulton Street, (212) 514-7182; in White Plains, in The Galleria, 100 Main Street, (919) 328-4272. These stores do not accept telephone orders, so you must buy your tickets in person.

Tickets By Phone

For ticket availability and to purchase tickets, call Ticket Master at any of the following phone numbers: (212) 307-1212, (201) 507-8900, (518) 476-1000, (914) 454-3388, (203) 525-4500, (609) 520-8383, (516) 888-9000, (203) 624-0033. You will pay a $3 shipping and handling charge for the entire order, and if you are ordering at least 9 days in advance, they will mail the tickets to you. Otherwise, you'll have to pick up your tickets before the game at the Paid Reservation Window next to Gate 4.

Tickets By Mail

If you want to order by mail, specify the date of game(s), the number of tickets, and the price. Make your check or money order payable to the New York Yankees, or if you're using a credit card be sure to include your credit card number and type of credit card. Add $2 to the total order for postage and handling. Mail your order to: Mail Order Dept., Yankees Ticket Office, Yankee Stadium, Bronx, NY 10451.

Tickets By Fax

Follow the mail order instructions above and fax your order to (718) 293-4841.

Cyber-Tickets

Visit www.yankees.com and surf your way to Yankees tickets. Also, check out their Stadium Seating Viewer, which gives you photo-like views of the field from various sections throughout the stadium.

Discounted Ticket Programs

The Yankees offer special ticket programs throughout the year, such as Senior citizen games ($2 tick-
ets), student-teacher games (half price), Tuesday
Night Out games ($9), youth and family games,
and free tickets for active military personnel.
Contact the Yankees at (718) 293-6000 for more
information.

Group Tickets

If you're able to organize a large group to attend a
game (25 or more fans), you should contact the
Yankees about a group package (718-293-6013).
Your group will receive 2 bonus tickets for every 25
paid tickets, preferred seating, and your group's
name in lights on the Stadium's centerfield mes-
sage board.

Yankee Stadium Ticket Exchange Policy

The Yankees do not allow you to exchange your
ticket, with the exception of rain-outs. If your game
is rained-out, you will be allowed to exchange your
ticket for the same priced seat either at the resched-
uled game or any other Yankees home game within
12 months of the rained-out game. Exchanges can
be made at Yankee Stadium or by mail (NY Ticket
Office, Yankee Stadium, Bronx, NY 10451).

Guided Tours

Guided tours are available year-round. Generally tours are Monday through Saturday at 12:00 noon. For groups of 12 or more, reservations are required. During the season (April through October) and when the team is in town, limited tours are available and clubhouse access is restricted. The cost for a Yankee Stadium tour is $8 for adults and $4 for children (14 and under) and senior citizens. If you have any questions regarding the tours, or would like to make a group reservation, call (718) 579-4531.

Early Bird Tip!

Once the playoffs end, it is time to start thinking about next season's tickets! For regular season tickets, the Yankees usually announce that tickets will go on sale in early December.

The Hazards of Buying From Scalpers

A trained eye can pick them out of the crowd. They almost always have an obnoxious, impatient expression and a snake-like demeanor. No, I'm not referring to Mets fans. I'm talking about scalpers. It is inadvisable to buy tickets illegally through scalpers because of the following possible pitfalls:

1. The scalper sells you tickets with incorrect date.

2. The scalper sells you a pair of tickets which are in different rows.

3. The scalper sells you lousy tickets in a supposed "dream location."

4. The scalper does not allow you to reconsider once you are holding the tickets and he has your money.

Note: It is also **illegal** to re-sell a ticket (even at face-value) once it has been purchased.

Picking the Best Place to Sit

While it is hard to find a bad seat anywhere in Yankee Stadium, here are some guidelines that will help you get the best seat possible. First, it is important to understand how the stadium seating is organized. There are 5 major groups of seats: the bleachers (behind the outfield), the Tier level (upper deck), the Loge level (middle deck), the Main level (lower level), and Field Boxes (closest to the field). With the exception of the bleachers, the sections are numbered in such a way that odd numbered sections are located along the first base and right field side, and even numbered sections are located along the third base and left field side of the field. This makes it pretty easy for you to figure out where you're sitting just by looking at the section number on your ticket.

Also, it is important to know what kind of a view you'll be getting when you buy your tickets. For all non-bleacher sections, the view from your seats will fall into one of four categories: (a) "home plate views," (b) "infield views," (c) "neck-benders," and (d) "outfield views." "Home plate views" put you right behind home plate, which is great if you like to watch the pitcher-hitter confrontation. The downside is that you are likely to watch the game through a protective net, since hitters often foul off pitches directly behind home plate. "Infield views" are probably the best view of all, because it gives you a great view of the entire infield and outfield, and is a good spot to snare foul balls. "Neck-bender" seats are named because fans sitting too far past first or third bases must turn their head to the left or right to follow the action at home plate. After a few hours of turning your neck 90 degrees, you may want to schedule an appointment with your chiropractor. Finally, "outfield views" are located past either foul pole in the outfield. While these seats are the farthest away, they are angled nicely towards the infield diamond, unlike the "neck-bender" seats.

Bleachers

$8 – Perhaps the most jovial section of Yankee Stadium, it is mostly populated by young, rowdy fans interested in harassing opposing pitchers (in the bulllpen) and opposing outfielders. These seats are the farthest from home plate (and thus farthest from the majority of the action), but fans enjoy this section for its fun-loving atmosphere and panoramic view of Yankee Stadium. The bleachers are great on warm summer days, but because there is no shade, be sure to bring some sunscreen. If rain

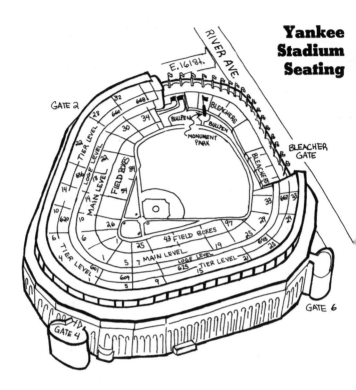

Yankee Stadium Seating

is a possibility, remember that you will be completely exposed to the elements.

The bleachers are split into two parts, one group of seats behind left-centerfield, and another group of seats behind right field. The center portion of the bleachers was covered to provide hitters with a better hitting background. The left side of the bleachers – called the "second bleachers section" – is further from homeplate than the right side, because Monument Park and the bullpens separate this part of the bleachers from the outfield. Despite the presence of the monuments and the bullpens, fans still have an unobstructed view of the field. The seats in this section, however, are not always sold, but are usually made available on special days, for special groups, or if the game is a complete sellout. The right side of the bleachers (sections 37-43) is closer to homeplate, and is home to the "bleacher creatures" a group of fans known for their extreme rowdiness and loyalty to the Yankees.

There are some drawbacks to sitting in the bleachers. First, you won't have a great view of the Stadium's main scoreboard (which resides behind and above the bleachers), although fans in the bleachers can follow the game by viewing the auxiliary scoreboards above first and third bases. Second, the bleachers section – true to its name – contains steel benches, so if you're looking for a comfortable seat with a seat-back, this is the wrong section for you. Third, the seats are not reserved, so you'll have to fend for yourself in finding a spot to sit. Finally, the bleachers are isolated from the rest of the Stadium, so if you want to walk around and take in the many angles of Yankee Stadium, you'll find the bleachers too confining. Of course, you can't beat the price!

Tier Reserved Seats

$14 – The highest possible spot to sit in at Yankee Stadium, these seats offer unobstructed views of the entire field. Also, you'll be completely exposed to the elements.

Home plate views: sections 1-8
Infield views: sections 9- 20
Neck bender views: sections 21 - 30
Outfield views: sections 31 - 36

Tier Box Seats

$23 – This section is the lower portion of the upper deck. Because you're paying $9 more than the Tier Reserved seats, you should make sure you're getting a seat that's in one of the lower rows in the section. Otherwise it's a better deal to buy a ticket in the Tier Reserved section, which may only be a few rows higher. Like the Tier Reserved seats, you'll be exposed to the elements.

Home plate views: sections 601-616
Infield views: sections 617 - 640
Neck bender views: sections 641 - 660
Outfield views: sections 661 - 670

Loge Box Seats

$29 / $26 – The Loge level offers a great view of the action, as it is closer to the field than the Tier level.

This section is pretty much sheltered by the Tier Level seating, so you won't get much sun sitting in this area. You'll stay dry, however, if it drizzles.

Home plate views: not available to the public
Infield views ($29): sections 420 - 474
Neck bender views ($26): sections 475 - 526
Outfield views ($26): sections 527 - 548

Main Reserved Seats

$26 / $23 – The Reserved section is the closest you can get to the field without sitting in a box seat. You'll be close to the action, but because this section is located below the loge level you won't get much sun.

Home plate views ($26): sections 1 - 8
Infield views ($26): sections 9- 20
Neck bender views ($23): sections 21 - 30
Outfield views ($23): sections 31 - 36

Main Box Seats

$29 / $26 – This section gets you close to the field and enables you to enjoy the outdoors without sitting in the shadow of the loge and tier levels above.

Home plate views ($29): sections 201- 228
Infield views ($29): sections 229- 280
Neck bender views ($26): sections 281 - 330
Outfield views ($26): sections 331 - 350

Field Box Seats

$ 29 – You have truly scored if you have these tickets. These seats are the closest to the field, and give you a chance to really experience the sights and sounds of the game. Of course, if you can't get these seats you can always sneak down to this section in the late innings of a game.

Home plate views: sections 1- 24
Infield views: sections 25 - 82
Neck bender views: sections 83 - 118
Outfield views: sections 119 - 136

Standing Room Only

The Yankees do not have a standing room only area.

Alcohol-Free Sections

For those of you who would like to sit in an alcohol-free zone, buy your tickets in sections 29, 31, 33, or 35 on the Loge Level, or in sections 8 and 9 on the Tier Reserved Level.

Handicapped Seating and Access

Yankee Stadium offers seating specifically designed for wheelchairs. These sections are located on the field level, rows K, Boxes 1-12. Also, seating is available in Reserved sections 2, 7, 8, and 10. Handicapped elevators are located in Sections 15 and 22.

How to Drive to Yankee Stadium

Driving to Yankee Stadium is pretty simple. Yankee Stadium is located in the Bronx at 161st St. and River Ave. If you're driving northbound on I-87, take exit 4 (149th St.) or exit 5 (155th St.) Driving southbound on I-87, take exit 6 (161st St). Once you've exited you'll see signs to the Stadium.

Parking Guide

Your best option is to park in any of the Kinney Parking Lots, which are scattered around Yankee Stadium. These lots cost $6 and allow you to park your car without fear of it being boxed-in, vandalized, or stolen. The latest time to pick up your car is 2 hours after the final pitch of the game. You will find Kinney Lots in the following locations (please see parking map), along with star ratings indicating how close the lots are to the stadium:

★★★

1. River Ave. at 71 E. 153rd St. (handicapped parking available)

2. River Ave – East 158th St. & East 157th St.

3. East 157th St. – River Ave. & Gerard Ave.

4. River Ave. – East 157th St. & 153rd St. (valet parking available)

★★

5. East 153rd St. at River Ave.

6. Exterior St. at Market Area

7. East 161 St. – Jerome Ave. & Macombs Dam Bridge

★

8. Jerome Ave. – East 164 St. & East 162nd St.

9. River Ave. at East 151st St.

10. River Ave. – East 151st St. & East 150th St. (2 locations)

11. River Ave. – East 164th St. & East 165th St. (Bus lot)

Rating Key
★★★ Yankee Stadium connoisseur's choice
★★ Seasoned Yankee fan's pick
★ Only under extreme time duress

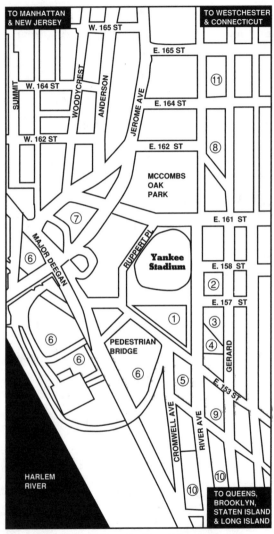

Yankee Fan's Parking Guide

Alternatives to Driving

If you don't want to deal with the hassle of driving (or if you're an ardent environmentalist), you have three alternatives to driving.

Subway

If you don't mind taking the subway, you can get to Yankee Stadium on several different subway lines. A trip from downtown Manhattan takes less than 25 minutes. The Yankee Stadium subway stop is located right outside the Stadium at the corner of 161st St. and River Ave. The #4 train (east side) as well as the C (west side weekdays only) and D trains (west side) make stops at 161st St./Yankee Stadium. Metro North train service to Connecticut and Westchester County is available at the 125 St. subway stop. (See the subway map on page 36).

Buses

Several New York City Transit Authority Bus Lines provide convenient service to Yankee Stadium. The BX 6, BX 13, and BX 55 buses stop at 161st St./Yankee Stadium. Also, the BX 1 bus stops at 161st St./Grand Concourse, a short walk from the Stadium. For more information on subway and bus transportation to Yankee Stadium, contact the NYC Transit Authority at (718) 330-1234 between 6am and 9pm.

Ferry

If traveling by sea is your thing, you can take a ferry from Manhattan or New Jersey to Yankee Stadium. For information and ferry schedule, call 1-800-53-FERRY in Manhattan or 1-800-BOAT-RIDE.

SUBWAY MAP

What to Bring

Observe the weather conditions, dress appropriately, and bring the necessary extras such as a wind-breaker for windy, colder weather, an umbrella in case of rain, and sunscreen on sunny days. Sporting white and blue garments will reinforce your Yankees loyalty, as will wearing a Yankees hat or T-shirt. Since you will most likely be sitting in the "common-man" areas, don't wear expensive, silk garments, because spilled bear or mustard are facts of life at any ball park. Small children and infants should be wrapped in swaddling Yankees colors. Sun-glasses (and regular glasses) are a plus, as are opera glasses or binoculars. You are allowed to bring a camera, so if it's convenient, bring it and capture Yankee Stadium's colorful charm. Be careful about bringing too many things, however, as there is very little room in front of and under your seat. One last thing...make sure to bring this guide!

What Not to Bring

First, avoid wearing hats and/or paraphernalia from other baseball teams (especially the Red Sox). Harmless as it may seem, you risk being harassed by Yankee fans in your section. Also, there are several items which Yankees security will not allow you to enter with: cans, bottles (glass or plastic), jugs, coolers, or hard containers of any kind. If you're bringing a lunch, Yankee Stadium security may search your bags and ask you to leave cans and bottles behind.

Rules on Banners and Signs

If you want to bring a sign or banner to the game, make sure that you don't hang it in any part of fair territory, or obstruct the views of other fans (even Rod Sox fans). Also, you will not be allowed to parade through the general seating areas between innings with your sign. Finally, your banner will be confiscated if you use any kind of weight to keep it in place.

How to Woo Your Woman into Letting You Go to the Game (For Men Only)

Men, you all know how hard it can be to unshackle that ball and chain from your leg and get out to the Stadium. But that's the price you pay for love! Whether it's your girlfriend, fiancee, or wife, try these proven techniques which will produce measurable results for you:

PLAN A: Walk in the house/apartment and pretend that she's already agreed to go to the game. Stride in confidently, and while hurriedly changing your clothes, remark, "OK, honey, are you almost ready to go to the game?" This technique works most effectively if she has a poor memory.

PLAN B: If Plan A fails, imply that some commitment exists, one which would be difficult to break. "But honey, the Johnsons have already planned to go with us." Or, "Dear, I already bought the tickets over the phone!"

PLAN C: If Plans A and B have failed, it's time to really put on the charm. Try sweet cooing noises in her ear, followed by an innocent, "Please, can't we go to the game tonight?" in a baby-like quiver.

PLAN D: If Plan C doesn't work, you're going to have to make some sacrifices. Promise to take out the garbage, iron the shirts, wash the dishes, or any other chores that need to be done when you return from the game (Don't worry, when you get back from the game, simply collapse in bed and feign a heavy sleep).

PLAN E: If she won't go for Plan D, try relating to her a poignant childhood story of when your dad took you to your first game at Yankee Stadium, and allow your voice to "choke up" a bit (Attempting this technique while dicing onions is most effective).

PLAN F: If she complains that the game is just too boring, assault her with a flurry of rebuttals, such as citing the great weather, or the current Yankees winning streak. Entice her with a delicious "dinner out" before the game (Wink wink: it will be those great sausages outside Yankee Stadium!). You can also try, "Honey, we don't have to stay for the whole game" (cross fingers behind back). If all else fails, try the line, "Don't you enjoy my company anymore?" with your head cocked at a pitiful angle with sad puppy eyes.

PLAN G: If nothing has worked up to now, you're in trouble. Drop to your knees, grab her legs and feet, and start begging. Don't let go until she gives in.

How to Leverage Your Position of Power With Your Man (For Women Only)

So, your man is always harassing you about letting him go to sporting events. But shackling him in the house isn't the answer. You must use a two-pronged strategy:

1. Go to a game with him. If you're already a fan, treat yourself to a night out in the fresh air and enjoy just being together. If you're not yet a fan, go anyway! You will gradually learn to love baseball, and actually enjoy the outings. How do you become a baseball fan? Well, by reading this book cover to cover, you'll know more about Yankee Stadium than he does. Start reading the sports section of the newspaper (in private, of course!), and various sports magazines such as Sports Illustrated. Also, watch the sports segment of the evening news. If you're puttering around the house, listen to the Yankees on the radio.

2. And now the more critical part: pretend you are not really that big of a sports fan, but are joining him because you love him so much! This allows you to leverage your power position — you are in the driver's seat now! The way to do this is through the magic of...

...THE POINT SYSTEM!!

Even if you are a fan, you can still pretend you're not up for it (headache, long day at work, weather, etc.). Every time you "do him a favor" by going to the game, assign a certain number of points to this favor (the two of you will agree on this number each time), and you'll find that it can become quite large when the Yankees are playing the Red Sox, or the weather outside is gorgeous. Now that you've agreed on the value of the favor, get it in writing. Create a table of favors, with various point values for each favor. Whoever has fewer points owes the other favors.

If the game is worth 3 points, for example, and he's in the red for three games (total of 9 points owed), think of all the great things he has to do for you! With his pas-sion for sports, you'll probably always be on the receiving end. And he won't resent you for these favors because, after all, it is you who is allowing him to go to the game!

Sample Point Sheet

Back rub ....2 points
Paint toe nails................2 points
Do dishes ....1 point
Treat dinner out.............3 points
Flowers all week............5 points
Girls night out ....4 points

CHAPTER THREE

PLAY BALL!

Pre-Game Activities

O n radio station WABC 770 AM, there is a pre-game show 30 minutes before the game, with players and the Yankees manager interviewed in the show. Tailgate barbecuing is not an option because you will most likely be parked in tightly with other cars and won't have room for a barbecue (save this for a Giants or Jets game!) If you want to have a snack, a drink, or a meal before the game, here are some suggestions:

Eat in the Park

The absolute best pre-game activity is getting into the park early, munching on some Yankee Franks, and taking in batting practice. The food inside the park is decent, and reasonably priced. Besides, the true baseball fan eats ball park food, not fancy restaurant cuisine!

If you don't want to eat in the park and decide to pass on the many outdoor food vendors, here are a few recommended eateries surrounding the Stadium:

Sidewalk Café

Located just outside the stadium between Gates 4 and 6, this enclosed area is a nice place to have a bite to eat. The café opens at 11 am on day games, and 5pm on night games.

Billy's Stadium Sports Bar

Located on River Ave. across the street from the Stadium. Sports Bar with typical sports bar food.

Stan's Sports Bar and Restaurant

Also located on River Ave. Typical sports bar food.

Ball Park Sports Bar & Grill

Located further down River Ave. Sports bar food combined with a souvenir shop and bowling lanes.

Yankee Tavern Food & Drink

Located about a block from the Stadium at the corner of E. 161st and Gerard. A fun place to eat before or after the game. Lots of Yankee memorabilia such as photographs of Yankee greats, and big, colorful murals of stars such as Ruth, Gehrig, and DiMaggio.

Yankee Pizza

Located on E. 161st between Gerard and Walton. A small pizza shop with decent pizza and calzones.

Court Deli Restaurant

Located at the corner of E. 161st and Walton. A typical NY Deli.

Monument Park

No trip to Yankee Stadium is complete without a pre-game visit to Monument Park (see Characteristics of Yankee Stadium, page 58). Monument Park, located behind the left field fence, contains stone plaques dedicated to former Yankee greats such as Babe Ruth, Lou Gehrig, and Joe DiMaggio. Monument Park is open from the time the Stadium gates open, and up until 45 minutes prior to game time. To visit Monument Park, go to section 36 between the Field and Main Level seats, and take the staircase to Monument Park.

Getting into the Stadium

"Whew, I thought we would have to call in the fire department, my team's so hot." – Casey Stengel, after his NY Mets snapped a 17-game losing streak.

You can enter the park up to an hour before game time (Monday through Friday) and up to 2 hours prior to game time on Saturdays, Sundays and holidays.

If you're sitting in the bleachers, the Stadium entrance is located on River Ave. For fans sitting along the third base line of the Stadium, enter through Gate 2 on 161st Street. For fans sitting behind home plate or along the first base side of the Stadium, enter through Gates 4 and 6 which are located on 157th and Rupert Streets. See stadium map on page 26.

Taking Care of the One You Love — Your Stomach

Find your seat first — then get your food. There is nothing worse than staggering through crowded sections of the park, arms full of teetering sodas and food, with your ticket in your mouth, trying to find your row ("excuse me, pardon me..."). It is also unpleasant for the other people you are disturbing.

There are food concession stands scattered throughout the Main, Field, Loge, and Tier levels, which offer the standard ballpark menu (beer, soda, hot dogs, pretzels, and other snacks). If you're looking for more variety, you can seek out the following concession stands: If you're sitting in the main or field level, you will find a food court (similar to standard ballpark menu but also offers specialty sausage, TCBY Yogurt, deli sandwiches, pizza, hamburgers, cheeseburgers, french fries, chicken fingers, nachos, and imported beer) along the left field side of the Stadium. You will also find a pasta and pizza stand, a soft ice cream stand, and a specialty sausage stand along the right side of the Stadium behind the Yankees dugout. Also, on the Tier level you will find, in addition to the many standard menu concession stands, an imported beer stand behind home plate. You will also find a stand behind the visitor's dugout that offers chicken fingers, hot dogs, sausage, hamburgers, french fries, and soda and beer.

Yankee Stadium Beer Rules

If you like to drink a few beers during a ball game, you should become familiar with "the beer rules." Study them, commit them to memory, for they shall govern your consumption at Yankee stadium.

Rule 1: Thou Shalt buy only two beers at a time in the bleachers.
Rule 2: Thou Shalt not buy a beer without identification.
Rule 3: Thou Shalt not buy beer at the start of the 7th inning or two hours into the game.
Rule 4: Thou Shalt not drink beer in Sections 8 and 9.
Rule 5: Thou Shalt not consume too much beer and be removed by security.

General Information

Telephones
Located on each side of the Stadium, and on every level

Men's/Ladies Rooms
Located on each side of the Stadium, and on every level

Customer Service Booths
Located on the Field Level behind Sections 2,9, and 33; on the Main Level behind Section 3; on the Loge Level behind Section 7; on the Tier Level behind Section 4.

Souvenir Stands
Six souvenir stands and two gift shops are located throughout the main and field levels. On the Loge Level there are four souvenir stands, but no gift shops. On the Tier level, there is one souvenir stand behind home plate.

Designated Driver Booth
If you volunteer to be your group's designated driver, go to section 4 on the Field Level and you'll receive coupons for free sodas!

First Aid
Located in Section 2 on the Field Level, and in Section 15 on the Main Level.

Lost and Found

Located in the Yankee executive office behind home plate.

ATMs

Two ATMs are located along the right side of the Stadium (section 9 behind the Yankee dugout) and along the left side of the Stadium (section 20 in shallow left field).

Following the Game

During the course of a game you will discover several areas of the stadium which provide information on player statistics, the score of the game, the scores of other games in progress, and the current number of balls, strikes, and outs.

There are two auxiliary scoreboards above first and third bases. The illustration below shows these scoreboards during a game between the Yankees and Indians. The scoreboards show the number of runs scored by each team, the number of the player currently batting, balls, strikes, outs, and the inning.

CLE	NY	AT BAT	BALLS	STRIKES	OUT	INN
2	5	42	3	1	1	7

Three main scoreboards, located in center and right fields behind the bleachers, show the scoring by inning, as well as player statistics and Diamond Vision replays.

Characteristics of Yankee Stadium

Dimensions

Much like Fenway Park, Yankee Stadium possesses its own unique geometry. Yankee Stadium's dimensions are 314 feet to the right field foul pole, 385 feet to right center, 408 feet to to center field, 399 feet to left center, and 318 feet to the left field foul pole. These current dimensions are radically different than those of "Old Yankee Stadium." Prior to the 1976 renovation, the left and right field foul poles were much closer (301 feet and 296 feet respectively), while the outfield dimensions were much greater. Most notably, "Old Yankee Stadium" featured very deep center field and left-center field dimensions of 457 feet and 461 feet respectively. Deep left and center fields were nicknamed "Death Valley" as many sluggers watched in dismay as their well-struck drives died there.

Another current Yankee Stadium quirk is the asymmetrical dimensions of the outfield fence, which is 8 feet high in left field, 7 feet high in left-center and center fields, 9 feet high in right-center field, and 10 feet high in right field. The Yankees claim that the fence is designed correctly, but that the field slopes and causes the fence to have various heights.

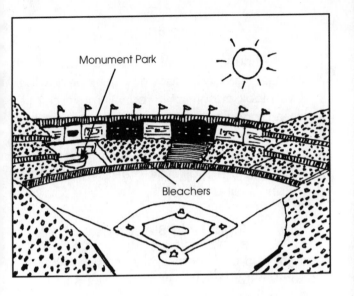

Monument Park

Bleachers

Architectural Touches

Yankee Stadium's cathedral windows on the outside give the Stadium a cathedral-like quality. This is consistent with the notion that witnessing a game at Yankee Stadium is indeed a religious experience. The beautiful arched art-deco frieze, which originally resided along the stadium roof facade, was removed but a portion hangs above the center field bleachers.

The Bat

Located outside in front of Yankee Stadium, this 120 foot high boiler stack has a unique flair to it. If you look closely at it you will make out the resemblance to an upside-down baseball bat. In fact, the smokestack has been modified to look just like a gigantic Louisville Slugger bat, including the manufacturer's seal and the Babe's signature.

Right Field Bleachers

The right field bleachers are as integral to Yankee Stadium's history as any other part of the ball park. Back in the 20's and 30's the bleachers were nicknamed "Ruthville" and "Gehrigville," due to the sluggers' propensity to hit titanic home runs into the crowd of crazed bleacher fans. The once enormous right field bleachers section has changed over the years, and now has a concrete base (vs. wooden) and is much smaller in size.

Bullpens

Located in left field, these bullpens have seen some of the greatest pitchers in baseball history warm up their golden arms. Legend has it

that Yankee starting pitcher Whitey Ford would arrange for a table with a full-course dinner to arrive in the bullpen. The ever confident Ford explained that since his fellow relievers would not be getting any work during the game (he assumed, of course, that he would pitch the entire 9 innings), they should at least enjoy themselves.

Monument Park

Monument Park honors great Yankees players and managers. A virtual museum of Yankees history, Monument Park allows fans to view the three original stone monuments of Ruth, Huggins, and Gehrig, as well as a fourth which was added to honor Mickey Mantle. Numerous plaques have been added to honor Ed Barrow (early general manager who converted Ruth from a pitcher into an outfielder), Jacob Ruppert (the great Yankee owner who started the club's dynasty), Joe DiMaggio, Casey Stengel, Joe McCarthy, Pope Paul VI, Thurman Munson, Pope John Paul II, Billy Martin, Whitey Ford, Left Gomez, Roger Maris, Allie Reynolds, Elston Howard, Phil Rizzuto, Bill Dickey, and Yogi Berra. Do not leave Yankee Stadium without visiting this special place.

Yankee Fans

Adjectives often used to describe Yankee fans are: insane, knowledgeable, partisan, scary, vulgar, ruthless. Your Yankee Stadium experience is incomplete until you see, hear, feel, and perhaps even smell the will of Yankee fans. During a Yankee rally, the fans will cheer until the rafters shake, stomp their feet in the bleachers, and generally rock "The House That Ruth Built." People drawing the ire of Yankee fans include visiting players, umpires who have the gaul to make calls against the home team, and visiting fans stupid enough to wear their team paraphernalia (particularly Boston fans). The hair-raising scenario of Yankee Stadium promoting "Bat Night" (during which the first 30,000 or so fans receive a free bat) has actually occurred. Yankee fans are bad enough without weapons. Perhaps Yankee Stadium should have a "Hand-cuff Night" or "Sedative Night" instead.

Famous Spots

Right Field Bleachers

Three historically-important home run balls have landed in the right field bleachers. The first occurred on September 30th, the last day of the 1927 season, when Babe Ruth hit his 60th home run of the season. The ball landed in the first row in the right field bleachers, just fair. The record 60th home run would stand for 34 years.

The second home run occurred on October 1st, 1961, when Roger Maris broke one of baseball's sacred records. Maris took Red Sox pitcher Tracey Stallard's offering and launched it into box 163D of right field's section 33. Mari's 61st home run was controversial for several reasons. First, many fans did not deem Maris worthy of breaking Ruth's record, and would have preferred Maris' more popular teammate Mickey Mantle to break the mark. Second, Maris' home run record would become saddled with the dreaded "asterisk," since his 61 homeruns had been hit in 163 games versus Ruth's 154 games.

The third home run occurred 2 years later on May 22, 1963. On a pitch from Kansas City's Bill Fischer, Mickey Mantle rocketed the ball high in the air and off the right field facade. Had the ball been hit just 6 inches higher, it would have cleared the roof and traveled an estimated 620 feet. It also would have been the only fair ball ever hit out of Yankee Stadium.

Infield

Of the many player appreciation days in Yankee Stadium history, none were as poignant as Lou Gehrig Appreciation Day on July 4, 1939. Surrounded by 62,000 fans and by players from the Murder's Row team of 1927, Gehrig gave his "luckiest man on the face of the earth" speech. Gehrig died two years later from amyotrophic lateral sclerosis, now known as "Lou Gehrig's Disease."

Pitchers Mound

The pitchers mound in Yankee stadium has witnessed seven Yankee hurlers pitch no-hitters. In 1938, Monte Pearson no-hit Cleveland, followed by Allie Reynold's blanking of Boston in 1951. Perhaps the most dramatic no-hitter was thrown on October 8, 1956, by Don Larsen, who beat Brooklyn in the World Series with a perfect game (not hits and no walks). Yankee no-hitters returned in the 80's as Dave Righetti no-hit the Red Sox in July of 1983. Three Yankee no-hitters occurred in the 90's, as the one-armed Jim Abbott (1993), Dwight Gooden (1996) and David Wells (1998) turned the trick.

Home Plate

No discussion of famous spots in Yankee stadium would be complete without mentioning home plate. Of course, Ruth's 60th and Maris' 61st homeruns qualify. Joe DiMaggio's 56 game hitting streak began at homeplate in May of 1941. Perhaps the most spectacular performance at the plate occurred during the 1978 World Series, as Reggie Jackson hit three consecutive homeruns on three pitches from three different Los Angeles Dodgers pitchers. Mr. October's homeruns helped the Yankees win their first world championship since 1962.

Outfield

Three of baseball's greatest players patrolled the outfield for the Yankees. With Babe Ruth in right field, and Joe DiMaggio and Mickey Mantle in center field, the Yankees had at least one Hall-of-Fame outfielder in their outfield for almost five decades.

Yankee Stadium Favorites

Yankee Stadium Sights

- Walking from the far corner of left field (next to Monument Park) to the far corner of right field. Taking in the various vantage points of the game as you work your way to right field.

- Participating in the "Wave," which usually starts in the bleachers, and almost always travels clockwise through the bleachers, into right field, and on through to left field.

- Watching the manager and the umpire arguing, escalating to the point where both are less than an inch apart, spraying saliva on each others faces, and always yelling at the same time.

- Watching the cleaning crew primp and preen the infield dirt and mound between the 5th and 6th innings.

- Watching beach balls ricochet around the bleachers, or even better, being in the bleachers and striking one of the balls.

- Watching the grounds crew covering the field during a rain delay.

- Witnessing the crowd's and players' reaction to a squirrel or a rat racing across the outfield.

Yankee Stadium Sounds and Smells

- The home plate umpire howling or grunting a called third strike on a bewildered batter.

- The crescendo of the crowd cheering as a well struck ball rises majestically over the outfield fence and into the bleachers for a home run.

- The National Anthem, and "Take Me Out to the Ball game" (sung during the 7th inning stretch).

- The combination of mustard, hotdogs, fresh air, cigar smoke, bubble gum, and roasted peanuts: a unique scent only found in baseball parks.

- The smell of the leather of a baseball glove that you've brought to track down foul balls.

- The smell of sizzling sausages outside of Yankee Stadium at the vendor carts.

Talk Like a Fan

"Whenever I decided to release a guy, I always had his room searched first for a gun. You couldn't take any chances with some of those birds." – Casey Stengel

I f you really want to be part of the "Yankee Stadium faithful," you need to master the slang, the delivery, the attitude of a true Yankee fan. The basic idea is to be wildly biased towards the Yankees, wildly opposed to the other team, and fickle with the umpires. Booing should be reserved for members of the other team, and only under extreme conditions is it acceptable to lay your wrath on a Yankee player. Extreme condition example: The Yankee clean-up hitter has not hit a home run in 2 months, is hitting below .200, has stranded 6 runners in the game thus far, and has just struck out with the bases loaded with the Yankees down by 2 runs.

Slang

Mastering Yankee Stadium fanhood also involves the use of baseball slang. Mastering the New York accent can take years of practice and is almost impossible to imitate properly by the novice. Your correct usage of words and expressions, however, will allow you to feel at home with the established "Yankee Stadium Faithful" in your section.

Guide to Yankee Stadium Slang

Slang	What it Means	Secondary Meaning
Aspirin tablet	fastball	cure for hangover
Baltimore chop	weak hit chopped off front of plate	imitation of Atlanta fans
Banjo Hitter	poor contact, makes sick sound	musician at bat
Batting practice pitch	weak, easy-to-hit fastball	pitch thrown during practice
Beanball	pitch which hits the batter	edible pitch
Boot	fielding error	for illegally-parked car
Bridge Master	pitcher who allows too many homeruns	card-game genius
Brush back	pitch intentionally thrown close to batter	a shower activity
Bum	lousy player (used liberally for pitchers)	a person's underside
Bush league	lacking class (minor leaguer)	league for ex-presidents
Cheese	fastball	edible mold
Chump	bum — used primarily for hitters	cousin of the chimpanzee
Comebacker	ball hit back at pitcher	boxer who keeps getting up
Cookie	an easy to hit pitch (see batting practice pitch)	a cute name for significant other
Cup of coffee	brief stint in majors with a team	morning drug
Dinger	homerun	hitting head on car door
Ducks on the pond	runners on base to be driven in	Central Park sight
Duster	brushback	household tool
Eephus pitch	10-12 feet in air, blooper pitch	no secondary meaning
Flake	eccentric player (pitcher)	dandruff
Gas	good fastball	result of a Yankee Stadium hot-dog
Green light	freedom to swing	signals chaos in New York traffic
Hanging curve	curve that doesn't break /easy to hit	your belly after too many beers

Slang	What it Means	Secondary Meaning
Head-hunting	throwing at batters' heads	the pigeons above
Hill	mound	Anita's last name
Homer	homerun	Simpsons character
Hook	curve	popular Peter Pan movie
Hot corner	3rd base	street corner in red-light district
Long-ball	also a homerun	book by Longfellow
Meatball	easy-to-hit pitch	Italian delicacy
Mop-up	pitch in relief way behind	janitor's duty
No-no	a no-hitter	words used by girlfriend
Ohfer	hitless day	grunting noise indicating pain
Out pitch	pitch a pitcher depends on to get batter out	no secondary meaning
Payoff pitch	full count pitch	illegally-funded pitch
Punch and Judy hitter	well placed soft singles	puppet who can hit
Purpose pitch	pitch thrown at batter to intimidate	politically-correct pitch
Quail shot (dying quail)	weak hit dropping in front of outfielders	Murphy Brown's comments
Scroogie	screwball pitch	Ebeneezer's nickname
Sitting duck	runner is picked off, thrown out easily	ugly duckling's lazy brother
Southpaw	left-handed pitcher	left-handed dog
Spitball	doctored (Vaseline pitch, pine tar ball)	seen flying off Eifel Tower
Stiff	lousy player (used mostly for batters)	your lower back in bleachers
Tater	homerun	an American dinner treat
Texas league single	lofted weakly into shallow outfield	no secondary meaning
Twin killing	double play	bizarre murder case
Uncle Charlie	curve ball	your father's brother
Wounded duck	weakly hit pop-up	hunter's nightmare
Yakker	sharp breaking curve	a good joke
Yellow yammer	curve	yellow bird

Sure-fire Expressions

The use of short, colorful expressions is common among Yankee Stadium fans. They are used primarily to summarize or observe situations on the field. They are often filled with emotions such as awe, sarcasm, wonder, cynicism, panic, or anger. Here are a few examples:

When the hitter strikes out:

- Say to the person sitting next to you, "He whiffed!!" or "He was blown away!"

- Yell at the player as he walks back to the dugout, "See ya!" or "Sit down!" or "Back to the minors!"

When the opposing pitcher is pitching poorly:

- Say to the person sitting next to you, "He's being lit up!" or "He's being shelled/ shellacked/ knocked around!"

- Yell to the pitcher after a big hit, "Nice pitch, Stottlemyre!" or "Give him another cookie, Stottlemyre!"

- Also, signal to the bull pen by touching outstretched arm (like manager does when he requests a pitching change).

When a Yankee pitcher is wild:

- Say to the person sitting next to you, "He's all over the place!" or "He's got control problems!" or "He can't find the plate!"

- Yell to the pitcher as the count goes to 3 balls, no strikes, "Throw Strikes!"

When the opposing pitcher is removed from the game after a poor performance:

- Yell, "Sayonara!" or "Hit the showers," or "Back to the minors!"

- Sing along with organ, "Nah, Nah, Nah, Nah... Nah, Nah, Nah, Nah.... Hey, Hey, Hey... Goodbye!" (Raise beer while singing).

Opposing Managers

As you become a Yankee Stadium fanatic you will find yourself disliking the opposing team's manager. Managers come in all different shapes, sizes, and personalities. Here are some basic categories that the other team's manager will likely fall into:

Ex-Player

- Fiery, wishes he could pick up a bat and take a swing.
- Prone to throwing Gatorade jugs onto the field in anger.
- Often yells at and kicks dirt onto the umpire.

Gambler

- Manages on gut feeling, "rolls the dice" frequently.
- Goes against conventional wisdom.

Computer Man

- Too analytical.
- Has all kinds of charts and numbers.

Text-book Manager

- Too theoretical.
- Manages from the old book.

Sleeping Beauty

- Sleeps in the dugout, drools.

- Wakes up to call the bull pen, or to make the long walk to the mound (sleep walking?).

- Usually over the age of 55.

Captain Hook

- Removes starting pitchers too early.

- Shows no patience with his pitchers.

Dealing with Umpires

"Many fans look upon an umpire as a necessary evil to the luxury of baseball, like the odor that follows an automobile." – Christy Mathewson

Cardinal rule: Take any call against the Yankees as a personal affront to your intelligence and integrity. Your goal is to sway the umpire's allegiance to that of the Yankees.

Common Tactics Used with Umpires

- On a call against the home team, yell "Get some glasses!" or "Get your prescription changed!"

- Cheer on the Yankees manager as he argues with the umpire.

- If the other manager argues, yell, "Kick him out, ump!"

- On close pitches called against the Yankees, groan or boo the ump, even if you are 100 feet away in the bleachers.

- If the opposing catcher goes to the mound to confer with his pitcher, groan, boo and yell at the ump to break it up.

Doing the Wave

1. Cheer it on to nurture it at the beginning.

2. Make sure to stand up, throw hands and arms up, and yell loud incoherent things.

3. The wave should only travel from left to right field and around clockwise.

4. Don't start the wave too early in the game — wait until slow moments in the middle innings.

Special Rules for Dealing with Pitchers

- If the Yankees relief pitcher is one strike away from ending the game, stand and clap rhythmically with the crowd in anticipation of the last out.

- When a Yankee relief pitcher comes out of the bull pen to finish the game, bow and pay homage to encourage him if you are in the bleachers near the bull pen. You can also yell words of encouragement while he is warming up. For pitchers in the opposing team's bull pen, harass them and try to destroy their confidence. Relief pitchers are usually a mental wreck because they have to come into pressure-packed situations. They will always pretend they are cool and mean, but inside they're all frazzled.

- If any pitcher has a no-hitter (has not allowed any hits in the game), under no circumstances should you say the words "no-hitter" or directly acknowledge that the pitcher is doing this. It is bad luck, and will surely destroy the pitcher's karma.

CHAPTER FOUR

POST-GAME TIPS

I f you're not too tired after the game and are looking for some fun and food to occupy yourself while traffic dies down, here are some post-game suggestions:

Souvenirs

If you'd like to take some souvenirs home with you, you'll have plenty of options:

Stadium Souvenir Shops
Located behind section 24 near the food court, and behind section 23 next to the Sidewalk café, these shops offer an array of jerseys, hats, and other souvenirs.

Outdoor souvenir stands
These stands are scattered around the Stadium, and are a convenient but lower-quality alternative to the Stadium shops.

River Avenue Shops
A variety of shops scattered down River Ave. across from the Stadium (Stadium Souvenir, Stan's Sports World, Pro Cap Dugout, Stan the Man's Baseball Land, Ball Park Souvenirs).

Bowling

If you're so inclined, you can actually bowl a few frames at Ball Park Lanes, located on River Ave. across from the Stadium.

CHAPTER FIVE

LIFE BEYOND YANKEE STADIUM

(YES, IT DOES EXIST)

Alternatives to the Stadium: TV and Radio Coverage

When you're not at Yankee Stadium you can still follow the Yankees on TV for those important 3-game series against arch-rivals. You can catch most of the Yankees game on WNYW channels. Check your local TV listings for the correct station.

Another option is to listen to the game on the radio. There's nothing quite like the experience of imagining the play on the field as the radio announcer paints a picture for you. Moreover, it's great background music that you can listen to while you're doing other stuff. It's tough to remain on the edge of your seat for three hours if you're not at the park. That's why TV or radio work so well while you're doing other things.

Finally, you can find Yankees information on the internet. Just surf your way to **www.yankees.com.**

Norwich Navigators

A great alternative to Yankee Stadium is a trip to the Yankee's AA farm team, the Norwich Navigators. While the Columbus Clippers are the Yankee's AAA farm team, you'd have to travel all the way to Ohio to see the team. The Navigators, however, are in Connecticut, so you can make a trip without too much driving.

Watching a game at their ballpark, Dodd Stadium, is great because you're guaranteed a great seat (only 6,200 seats), it's cheap (most seats are $6), and you'll be away from all the hustle and bustle of the big leagues. There's even a picnic area where you can watch the game while lounging on your blanket.

Getting to Dodd Stadium is easy. From I-395 (which is just off I-95), take exit 82. At the bottom of the exit take a left (if traveling north on I-395) or a right (if traveling south on I-395). Take a right onto Norwich Industrial Park, and follow the green and white Dodd Stadium signs until you come to the stadium on the right.

Tickets are cheap. General admission seats are only $6 for adults, and $4.50 for children or seniors. Reserve seats are $7, and for you big spenders Premium Box seats are $9. To purchase tickets call 1-800-64-GATORS or visit www.gators.com.

Spring Training!

For those of you craving Yankees baseball by March, you might want to make a trip to Tampa, Florida and take in some games at Legends Field. This beautiful spring training facility holds 10,000 fans, offers tickets at a somewhat reasonable $10, and even sports a mini-Monument Park. The Yankees have been known to sell out all their spring training games, so if you're planning a trip to Florida, try to buy your tickets in advance.

Following the Yankees on the Road

For those of you who do a lot of traveling, you sure know the agonizing feeling of not being able to follow the Yankees, especially during a pennant race. Here are some suggestions for keeping up with the team:

1. Read the sports section in USA Today. It has the best sports coverage for the traveler, and you can usually find this newspaper anywhere, even overseas.

2. ESPN does good work each night showing highlights of the day's ball games. They also broadcast games several nights during the week. Given the Yankees' broad appeal throughout the country, you'll probably be able to catch a few Yankees games on ESPN no matter where you're traveling.

3. Try going to a baseball game in the city you're visiting. At least you'll be at the park, and all the stadiums show updated scores of all the games around the league so you can monitor the Yankees throughout the game. Sampling different parks and stadiums is a lot of fun, and makes you appreciate Yankee Stadium's unique qualities.

CHAPTER SIX

FANHOOD CHALLENGE

Multiple Choice Quiz

1. The "Old Yankee Stadium" featured a dark green screen which was used to:

    a. Shield the outfield fans from the sun or rain

    b. Honor St. Patrick's Day

    c. Give Yankee hitters an advantage over visiting hitters

    d. Prevent the blue outfield facade from clashing with the seats

    e. Help the grounds crew grow the grass to a dark green color

2. "The Monuments" of Ruth, Huggins, and Gehrig made it difficult for outfielders because:

    a. They were located in the outfield and could obstruct play

    b. Many outfielders were "spooked" by the historic plaques

    c. They cast a shadow over deep centerfield

    d. Visiting outfielders thought the monuments were actual teammates on the field

    e. They often toppled over and crushed helpless outfielders

3. Roger Maris hit his 61st homerun in:

   a. 1961

   b. 1927

   c. 1936

   d. little league

   e. 1967

4. The best way to order tickets on game day is to:

   a. Show up at Gate 6 and tell security that a Red Sox fan stole your tickets.

   b. Dress up in your Yankee uniform and go through the players entrance

   c. Look for scalpers

   d. Purchase them at the Advance Ticket Window

   e. Give up

5. "Death Valley" was named after:

   a. The visiting team's dugout

   b. Deep left/center field

   c. Craig Nettles' stinky locker

   d. Yankee Stadium bathrooms

   e. George Steinbrenner's Office

6. Yankee Stadium's smallest crowd of 413 fans occurred in:

    a. 1934 during World War II

    b. 1923 during Yankee Stadium's first year

    c. 1993 against the hapless Cleveland Indians

    d. 1966 against the White Sox

    e. 1952 after Mickey Mantle retired

7. If you must buy scalped tickets, you should:

    a. Attach a sign to your chest reading "Need to buy illegal tickets"

    b. Stand around looking for the slick-looking people murmuring "tickets, tickets"

    c. Ask a police officer where you buy the tickets from scalpers

    d. Turn hat inside-out

    e. None of the above

8. The Yankees prohibit the following items from being brought into the Stadium:

    a. Can of Sprite

    b. Bottle of root beer

    c. A cooler with your lunch in it

    d. An automatic weapon

    e. All of the above

9. The pitcher throws a 95 mph fastball close to the batter's face. This is called:

    a. A purpose pitch

    b. A scroogie

    c. A dinger

    d. An ohfer

    e. A spitball

10. Yankee Stadium was nicknamed "The House That Ruth Built" because:

    a. Ruth's cousin was it's construction foreman

    b. Ruth dictated its dimensions to team management

    c. Yankee Stadium was built by Ruth & Hamaker Construction

    d. It was built to showcase Ruth's talent

    e. The roof facade looked very similar to Ruth's childhood home

11. Casey Stengel's famous quote, "Ruth, Gehrig, Huggins, someone throw that darned ball in here, now!" occurred:

    a. When the three hall-of-famers were horsing around with a football in the locker room

    b. During an infield drill in spring training

    c. When a ball was hit into center field among the monuments

    d. After Stengel lost his cool during pre-game drills in the 1937 World Series

    e. During an amateur try-out for the three rookies

12. "Ruthville" and "Gehrigville" were named after:

a. The neighborhoods that Ruth and Gehrig lived in

b. The home dugout

c. Ruth's and Gehrig's lockers

d. Right and Left Field

e. The right field bleachers

13. During the 1974-1975 renovation of Yankee Stadium, the Yankees:

a. Played all their games on the road

b. Played their home games at nearby Shea Stadium

c. Cancelled the 1974 and 1975 seasons

d. Played their games in the Stadium, but no fans were allowed in

e. Reduced ticket prices to $1 for those fans willing to watch games amid the construction

ANSWERS

SCORING

0–3 correct	Lost Orioles Fan
4–7 correct	"Standing-room-only" peon
8–10 correct	Bleacher bum
11–13 correct	Yankee Stadium Connoisseur

Yankee Stadium Puzzle

Find the 14 hidden words.

```
M  T  B  R  O  N  X  R  K  S  R  Q  L
O  A  L  W  G  Q  O  B  G  W  K  S  E
N  K  X  B  C  D  G  U  P  C  B  T  Z
U  A  Y  L  U  B  A  L  L  K  L  R  J
M  Y  B  E  T  S  J  L  S  J  E  I  L
E  C  R  A  E  X  S  P  J  N  J  K  E
N  K  L  C  T  F  E  E  T  B  N  E  R
T  J  S  H  W  W  N  B  R  A  D  E  S
S  N  D  E  A  T  H  V  A  L  L  E  Y
B  T  M  R  N  M  O  R  H  U  H  P  O
R  F  I  S  C  O  W  D  U  G  O  U  T
U  C  S  K  K  U  S  I  T  E  M  F  A
W  U  E  E  G  N  P  N  R  H  E  Z  T
G  R  K  G  Z  D  B  G  E  J  R  V  E
L  V  L  B  A  G  L  E  K  T  J  O  R
A  E  R  B  A  B  E  R  U  T  H  X  P
```

Note: Waldo cannot be found in this puzzle.

ANSWER

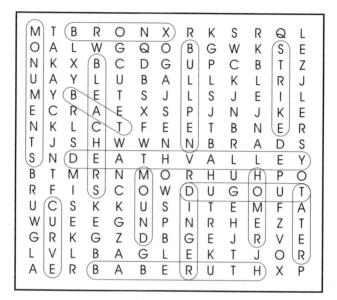

Yankee Stadium in Your Pocket Survey

Please fill out this survey and send it to us. If we use your feedback, we'll give you official recognition in the next edition of this book.

Name (optional): _____

Address (optional): _____

_____

_____

Gender: ❏M ❏F

Age range: ❏ under 18 ❏ 18–25 ❏ 26–40 ❏ 40+

What best describes you?
❏ local Yankee fan
❏ out of towner visiting the New York area
❏ other _____

Why did you buy the guide? (Check all that apply)
❏ souvenir of Yankee Stadium
❏ useful info on planning a trip to the Stadium
❏ fun stuff to read about the Yankees
❏ I didn't buy it, it was given to me as a gift
❏ other _____

How have you been using the guide? (Check all that apply)
❏ read once for fun and put away
❏ use to plan trips to Yankee Stadium
❏ take it with me to the game
❏ other _____

Please share your personal tips and secrets to enjoying a game at Yankee Stadium below. If we use your tips we will recognize you in the next edition of this book.

_____
_____
_____
_____
_____
_____
_____
_____
_____
_____
_____
_____

Please let us know if there's any way we can improve this guide. _____

_____
_____
_____
_____
_____
_____
_____
_____
_____

Thanks for your valuable input!

Mail survey to: Baseball Direct, P.O. Box 6463, Central Falls, RI 02863.